10/01

17.95

Everything You Need to Know About

LOOKING AND FEELING YOUR BEST

A Guide for Girls

What do you see when you look in the mirror? Read on to find out more about looking and feeling great!

• THE NEED TO KNOW LIBRARY •

Everything You Need to Know About

LOOKING AND FEELING YOUR BEST

A Guide for Girls

Annie Leah Sommers

THE ROSEN PUBLISHING GROUP, INC.
NEW YORK

Published in 2000 by The Rosen Publishing Group, Inc.
29 East 21st Street, New York, NY 10010

First Edition

Library of Congress Cataloging-in-Publication Data

Sommers, Annie Leah, 1968–
    Everything you need to know about looking and feeling your best: a guide for girls / Annie Leah Sommers.
        p.   cm.—(The need to know library)
    Includes bibliographical references and index.
    Summary: Explains the importance of good grooming, hygiene, nutrition, fitness, and attitude.
    ISBN 0-8239-3079-3 (lib. bdg.)
    1. Teenage girls—Health and hygiene Juvenile literature. 2. Beauty, Personal Juvenile literature. [1. Health. 2. Grooming. 3. Beauty, Personal.] I. Title. II. Title: Looking and feeling your best. III. Series.
    RA777.25.S67 2000
    613'.04243—dc21   99-16834
                                                                                                                    CIP

Manufactured in the United States of America

Contents

Introduction

We all know that growing up is a challenging process. As you get older, a lot of changes take place—changes that affect both your body and your mind. Figuring out how to deal with all the new things that are happening can be difficult. Since it's easier to cope with life when you are feeling your best, the first step is to learn *how* to feel your best.

To do this you need to be healthy and to have a positive self-image. When you are happy with who you are—how you look, how you feel, and how you act—you will feel more confident confronting the new and exciting world of being a teenager. By recognizing and understanding the importance of caring for yourself now, you also will be preparing yourself for a happy and healthy future.

This book aims to help you look and feel your best. You may not be aware of it, but everything you do—from what you eat (or don't eat) at breakfast to how much sleep you get to how often you wash your hair—has an effect on who you are and how others see you. This book discusses three important elements of looking and feeling your best: good grooming, or making yourself presentable; proper hygiene, or keeping yourself clean; and a healthy diet, or eating the foods you need to give you the vitamins, nutrients, and energy to grow.

This book also includes information on getting fit, dressing for success, and shopping sensibly. Even if you dread gym class, this book suggests plenty of other ways to stay in shape—even fun ones! You will learn about the importance of dressing appropriately as well as how to find fashionable clothing at low prices. The sections at the back of the book list Web sites, books, and organizations that can provide more information on topics ranging from nail care to being a vegetarian.

Césaria's Story

Césaria is in seventh grade. It takes her forty minutes to get to school on the bus that stops outside her house at 8 AM. Classes start at 8:45 AM, but since Césaria wakes up at ten minutes before 8:00 every morning, she barely has time to get ready for school.

When Césaria's mother asks her why she does not get up earlier, so that she can take a shower and eat breakfast with the rest of the family, Césaria replies that she likes to get her beauty sleep.

The girls at school laugh at Césaria when, day after day, she shows up wearing the same raggedy shirt and jeans. In class, Césaria slumps in her chair, barely able to keep her eyes open while everyone takes turns reading from Lord of the Flies.

"Phew!" says Ramona, walking by Césaria with one hand covering her nose. "Don't you ever wash?" she asks, fanning the air in front of her as though she smelled a skunk.

Césaria has a habit of twirling her finger in her long, unbrushed hair. Sometimes when she does this, her finger catches in the tangled mess. One day in math class, Césaria was trying to unwind some strands of hair from her finger when the teacher interrupted her.

"Césaria," called Ms. Robotic, "would you mind paying attention to what's on the blackboard rather than what's stuck in your hair?" Everyone in the class laughed, and Césaria turned bright red. Later that day, a girl named Rosa aimed a scrunched-up piece of paper at Césaria's head.

"Oh, sorry, Césaria," she said. "I meant to throw the note in the garbage can. I guess I got confused."

Rosa's friend Amy was next. She ran up to Césaria and shouted, "Smelly-pits-and-lots-of-zits!"

Césaria did have more frequent acne breakouts than most girls her age, but what could she expect, since she didn't take time to wash her face?

Césaria ignored her classmates' mean comments. She had no intention of changing her clothes more than once a week. And as for her hair, why should she bother brushing it every day, let alone washing it more than once every two weeks? Her favorite all-girl band had the same hairstyle as she did.

One morning, Césaria's mother, Tina, came into her

daughter's room at 7:30 holding a clean pair of jeans and a pretty lavender T-shirt. Césaria complained, but Tina firmly told her to get up and take a shower if she wanted to continue getting her allowance. After a lot of grumbling, Césaria gave in. Once in the shower, she noticed that the fresh scent of her brother's apple shampoo made her feel awake. The heat of the water from the shower felt almost as good as staying in bed until the last possible minute.

Since she felt so fresh and clean, Césaria decided to go one step further and brush her teeth. When she ran her tongue along her teeth, Césaria was amazed at how nice and smooth they felt.

After dressing quickly, Césaria noticed that she still had lots of time before her bus arrived. Césaria put on some deodorant and brushed out her tangled hair while her mother made her toast and eggs.

On the school bus, a cool guy in Césaria's math class said "hi" to her. Wow, Li Chu never said anything to me before, Césaria thought to herself. The day was off to a good start! When she was at her locker, Rosa waved to her and smiled. Even Ms. Robotic seemed happy to see Césaria. And interestingly enough, Césaria didn't slouch through any of her classes. She had lots of energy and felt much better than usual.

When Césaria went to the bathroom before lunch, she did something that was very rare: She smiled at her reflection in the mirror. She then decided that she would go home and do her laundry after school.

Back to Basics

Césaria is now a completely changed person. All she needed was a little reminder about the basics of good grooming. Somewhere along the way, Césaria had forgotten that a few good habits go a long way.

Some quick reminders about hygiene and health:

- Soap is your friend! Washing your face and body with soap and warm water keeps you smelling and looking good and helps to prevent against infections. If your skin is dry, oily, or combination (dry in some areas and oily in others), don't worry. There are many types of soaps to choose from that can clean your skin without irritating it. Don't forget to wash all over your body!

  You may want to use a different soap for your face than for your body if your facial skin is particularly oily or dry or if you get a lot of pimples and blackheads. There are creams and ointments available at drugstores that help dry up pimples and keep them from spreading. It is very important not to pick, pop, or squeeze your zits. When you do, you are spreading germs—and new pimples—to other areas of your skin. You could also be creating scabs that can leave scars.

- Try to brush your teeth at least three times a day with a toothpaste containing fluoride. This is especially important if you wear braces or a retainer, which can trap food particles in your mouth and lead to cavities if not properly cleaned. You might want to pack an extra tooth-brush and toothpaste with your lunch. Most drugstores sell small, inexpensive travel sets that are easy to carry.

Flossing is also important, as it cleans away the plaque that builds up in hard-to-reach places your toothbrush can't access. Dentists recommend replacing your toothbrush every three months so that the bristles don't wear down. Remember to have a dental check-up at least once a year. Proper care of your teeth will keep you from developing gum disease and halitosis (bad breath).

• Don't forget your daily dose of deodorant. No matter how well you wash, your body is still going to produce sweat, especially under your arms. You can choose from roll-on, spray, or stick deodorants; they come in a variety of scents, as well as unscented versions.

• Keep your hair healthy and happy. Your hair type—oily, dry, or a combination of both—and your lifestyle will dictate how often you need to wash and condition your hair. It's important to keep hair clean and relatively neat, especially for an important occasion like a job interview.

The next five chapters contain much more information about how to keep yourself looking and feeling your best, so turn the page!

Chapter 1

First Impressions Count

At some point in your life, your mother or father or even an older sibling has probably said something to you like, "Remember to brush your hair—first impressions are important." Or perhaps the phrase was "Why don't you put on a nice clean shirt? First impressions really count." It's likely that when you first heard these kinds of comments, you grumbled and responded, "Why? Do I really have to?" or "No one will notice the small toothpaste stain on this shirt." Maybe you complained and went right out the front door with pasta sauce on your jeans. Or maybe you agreed to wash your face, change your T-shirt, or comb your hair. Whatever choice you made, and whether or not you agreed with the advice you were given, take a moment to think about the following question: Can you honestly say that you have never looked at a stranger and formed an impression of him or her based only on how that person looked?

More likely than not, the answer is no. The truth of the matter is that we live in a society that places great emphasis on first impressions and appearance. That's why it is important to try to express yourself in a manner that will reflect well of you.

Erin's Bad Day

Erin wanted to get a part-time job after school. There was a Donut King close by, so she went in and filled out a job application form. Two days later Erin received a call from Seth, the Donut King manager. He wanted Erin to come in for an interview the next day at four o'clock. Erin hung up the phone and ran in to tell her sister, Glynnie, the good news.

"Oh, Glynnie, I'm so excited. I got a job interview tomorrow after school!"

"That's great, sis," replied Glynnie, barely looking up from her chemistry text. "What are you going to wear?"

"Oh, well, I bought a new dress at the Mall of America last week. Maybe I'll wear that."

"Sounds good, as long as it's conservative enough," said Glynnie.

"Oh yeah, sure. It's really conservative," Erin replied, barely able to contain her laughter.

She was sick of Glynnie and her conservative clothes. Glynnie was in college and was trying to get into medical school. All she did was read science books and wear button-down shirts and boring chino pants. Erin thought that Glynnie looked like someone's granny with her sensible shoes and crisply ironed shirts.

The last time Erin took Glynnie's advice on what to wear was when they had first moved to Minneapolis from San Jose, California. Glynnie had told Erin to "dress conservatively" on her first day of school, and stupidly, Erin had listened to her. Erin spent the whole day wanting to hide in the bathroom because she felt like such a nerd in her pleated skirt and penny loafers. All the cool kids, the ones hanging out in the cafeteria, were wearing black leather jackets and lots of makeup.

The next morning, Erin spent more time than usual getting ready so she'd look good at the interview. She teased her hair and put in lots of gel for a nice spiky effect. She made her face really pale, like the kids at the Goth coffee shop she liked to go to, and she drew thick black circles around her eyes with eyeliner. Then she carefully slipped the tight black dress over her head, grabbed her black leather jacket, and went out the door.

Erin didn't get the job at the Donut King. She barely even had a chance to say hello to Seth. As soon as she sat down and took off her jacket, Seth told her that it was a waste of his time to interview someone who "obviously had no idea how to dress appropriately." When she saw the disgusted look on Seth's face, Erin felt so rotten that she started crying. To make things worse, all of her eyeliner and mascara started to stream down her face!

The Pros and Cons of Snap Judgments

From Erin's experience, you can see that first impressions can have a very strong effect on people. Maybe now Erin will stop being so scornful of her sister and will try adding a few more presentable items of clothing to her wardrobe.

It is important to note, however, that snap judgments can often be inaccurate. Think about a few people that you know well. Do you remember the first time you saw them? Can you recall what they were wearing or what their hair looked like? Were they neat and pleasant looking or messy and unkempt? What did you think about them then? Did you know at once whether you would like them or not?

Let's go back to Erin's first day at her new high school. The kids she had initially wanted to be friends with were the ones that she thought looked cool. And why did she think they looked "cool"? Because they had certain things that Erin associated with being attractive and desirable (in this case, leather jackets and makeup). What if later on, Erin finds out that one of the "cool" girls is actually not a very nice person at all, regardless of the fact that she has a nice jacket and wears funky makeup?

You may now be wondering why it might *not* be a good idea for Erin to make snap judgments about who she wants to have as a friend, but it *is* okay for Seth to decide not to hire Erin before even talking to her. The important difference between these two situations is that Erin's choice of friends is a personal decision that involves only herself and her friends. Seth's choice of an employee affects not only Erin and himself, but also many other people.

When we enter a store—just like when we go to the bank, the post office, or the hair salon—we expect courteous and professional service. Employers want to hire people who are friendly, confident, and bright, with a likable personality and an appealing appearance. A customer who goes into Donut King and sees Erin with her dramatic white face powder, spiked hair, and low-cut, slinky dress may form a negative impression about the store based only on how Erin looks. If the customer assumes from Erin's appearance that the service will be unprofessional and rude, he or she may decide not to buy donuts. This will damage Seth's business. A child who is not aware of the latest fashion trends may even be scared by Erin. When you hold a job that involves interacting with the public, it is important to present an image that will be seen as agreeable by as many people as possible. With friends, on the other hand, it's okay to dress how you want (within limits!), even if your style may not appeal to everyone.

Seth did not say that Erin was a bad or mean person. He did not make a snap judgment about Erin's *character*. All he did was honestly state that Erin's appearance was not right for the job at Donut King.

Why We Judge People

If you are beginning to think that this whole first impression thing is superficial—that is, insignificant and petty—read on. There are important reasons why we form instant impressions of new people.

Believe it or not, we judge others for our own safety. A stranger we meet in a public place could turn out to be very dangerous. How the person is dressed, his or her facial expression, or the type of body language the stranger exhibits may give us clues. For example, imagine meeting a strange man in the park on your way home from school. If he is dressed like a member of a gang, or if he speaks abruptly and angrily and keeps staring at you, it would be a good idea to stay out of this person's way. In situations like this, you depend on your quick assessment and judgment to protect yourself.

Another reason we check people out is to keep our lives in order. We meet so many people over time that we need to use some kind of system of picking and choosing who we want to get to know and who will become important to us. When we act according to our instincts (unlearned reactions that come from within us), we do so in order to determine what is best for us. To find out who we would like to become friends with, or who we might have a good conversation with, or what shoes we want to buy, we make judgments about people, places, and things.

This instinctive judgment—usually our first judgment,

since we often reevaluate something later on—is based on our senses: what we see, hear, and smell. Suppose you need to study with someone for an upcoming Spanish test. Your teacher introduces you to Marcus, but when the two of you meet up at the library, you realize that you don't want to study with Marcus because you don't like the smell of his cologne. The next time you are supposed to meet with Marcus to go over verb tenses, you tell him that you are feeling sick.

We know that snap judgments aren't always accurate. You will need to know more about Marcus than the fact that you don't like his cologne to be able to fairly decide if he will be good at helping you with Spanish. However, it is easy to make snap judgments. And because of this, you need to pay close attention to how you appear, because others are going to be making the same kinds of judgments about you.

First Impressions: What Counts

If someone were to meet you for the first time, what would he or she be able to tell about you? Are you neat and tidy? Or are you messy and sometimes sloppy? Are your clothes right for the occasion? Do you look as though you care about your appearance? Are you dressed or groomed in a way that may offend some people? Do you look like you are into the latest trends?

Your appearance can also reveal a lot about your interests. If you wear jeans and boots and your skin is glowing with the color of a deep tan, someone might assume that you participate in a lot of outdoor activities. If you are wearing a style of clothing that is popular because a rock band dresses that way, people may guess that you are a fan of that particular band or type of music.

Your appearance is made up of many different elements. And how you feel is often reflected in how you look. If you lead a healthy lifestyle—one that includes eating well, drinking lots of water, and getting fresh air, exercise, and plenty of rest—you will look and feel good about yourself. And if you pay attention to how you look—keeping your hair, face, and body clean, and wearing flattering, comfortable clothing—others will treat you with respect and will feel good about you too.

Chapter 2

Attitude and Appearance

In the Introduction and in chapter one, we saw how both Césaria and Erin learned about the importance of paying attention to their external appearance, including choice of clothing, hygiene, and hair care. Your outward appearance, however, is not the only part of you that affects how you feel and how others may view you. Believe it or not, what goes on inside you also plays a significant role in your overall appearance.

Facial Expression

Do you know someone whose only facial expression is a frown? If you don't know this person very well, based on your first impression of him or her, do you think you will want to get to know this person better? Let's take a look at how facial expression can affect the way someone is viewed by those around her.

Happy

Sad

Lonely

Unfriendly

Annoyed

Friendly

Gaby

It was Tuesday morning and Gaby's mother, Agnes, was hard at work in the kitchen. She and her husband, Sebastian, woke up at 5 o'clock every morning to make fresh bread for their eight children. Gaby and the three youngest children were at the kitchen table. They were eating their cornmeal pancakes with freshly picked strawberries. Everyone but Gaby seemed to be enjoying the meal that had been prepared with so much love and care. Gaby was scowling and the food on her plate was untouched.

"Gaby," said Agnes, "is there something wrong with my cooking? You don't look like you are enjoying it at all."

"Eat up, my little peach," Sebastian added.

Gaby ignored her parents and left the table without a word. Agnes and Sebastian were hurt that Gaby did not appreciate their attempt to make breakfast a happy time.

Later that day, the students in Mrs. Munster's gym class were dividing into two teams for softball. Gaby stood behind the baseball diamond and practiced doing cartwheels. She wasn't paying any attention to what was going on with the rest of her class.

"Pick me, pick me!" shouted the students. Everyone was excited to play in the first game of spring. The winter had been long and it was nice to be outside in the sun, even if they were still at school.

Mrs. Munster looked around and spotted Gaby, who was now sitting on the ground staring at the clouds.

"Come and join us, Gaby," she called.

Gaby looked extremely bored. She gave Mrs. Munster a cold stare and walked silently toward the group of happy and eager students. She scowled at everyone who looked her way.

Based on Gaby's facial expression and attitude, what sort of impression or opinion would you form of her? What adjectives would you choose from the list below to describe what kind of a person you think Gaby is?

- angry
- happy
- unfriendly
- sad

- friendly
- depressed
- lonely
- fun

Since you have only known Gaby to wear a frown, a scowl, or no expression at all, you would probably describe her as anything but happy, fun, or friendly. It would not be mean or inaccurate to deduce—come to a conclusion based on past examples—that Gaby is unapproachable.

So what? you may be thinking. Leave her alone and let her be in a bad mood. In truth, there is nothing wrong with being in a bad mood. We all have moments when we feel down or blue. And Gaby may be dealing with a serious problem. There are times, however, when you might want to pay more attention to what is going on inside of you—and how this is being reflected in your outer appearance. This is especially true when you are interacting with others. How you feel inside relates to how you look on the outside. And though it is certainly true that some people are more expressive—showing their feelings or emotions—than others, there are consequences to having a certain facial expression.

For example, let's say that Gaby, along with two other girls, Amy and Edie, are all new students this year. Amy and Edie generally look upbeat and friendly. It would not be surprising if other students were more inclined to make friends with them instead of Gaby. Why? Because Amy's and Edie's expressions may lead others to believe that they are more welcoming and approachable than Gaby.

If Gaby knows and understands the importance of her facial expression and is aware that she tends to look unfriendly, she can start to make positive changes. For the moment, she may not even realize how she appears to others. Once she is aware of the impression she gives and the importance of facial expression, she can try to understand herself better. Then people will react to her with more understanding.

That is what happened with Césaria in the Introduction. It wasn't until Tina and the girls at school made it obvious to Césaria that her appearance was causing others to ridicule her that she decided to do something about it. Once she became aware of what she was doing—or, in her case, of what she wasn't doing—Césaria was able to take positive action.

There are situations in which it is very important to

control your facial expression. If you are the new kid at school, camp, a place of worship, or any organization, you may want to make an extra effort to look open and friendly. If, like Erin in chapter one, you are going to a job interview, it helps to look alert, interested, cheerful, and positive. Most of this is just common sense, but we often forget that the little details count too.

Verbal Expression

Martina met Chad in a club downtown. They danced for a while and then went outside and talked. Martina could barely stop looking at Chad. He was so cute. He had great eyes and high cheekbones. Chad didn't seem like a big talker—more like the silent, good-looking type. Martina was majorly crushing on him, so she asked Chad about his family to get the conversation rolling.

But when Chad started talking, Martina could not believe the words that were coming out of his mouth. He was so rude, her eyes nearly popped out of her head in disgust! Not only did he swear every second word, but from what he told Martina about his parents and his older sister, he had no respect for anyone. Besides, Martina could barely get a word in edgewise. Wow! How egotistical can you get? thought Martina. All of a sudden, Chad didn't seem so cute anymore.

Appearance Isn't Everything

You may not have realized this before, but how you are perceived by others is also affected by your speech and

Having an open, friendly face lets other people know that you
are a likeable person.

your verbal expression. We saw how Martina's impression of Chad went from extremely positive to the opposite end of the spectrum, or scale, once Chad expressed himself verbally. Excessive swearing and poor social skills—such as only talking about you, you, and you—will reflect poorly on you regardless of how nice your clothes are or how physically attractive you appear.

Chapter 3

You Are What You Eat

In chapter two, we learned how both your facial and verbal expressions can affect how others view you. This chapter focuses on the role of food in determining your physical appearance and your mental health. Of course, the features that you were born with are the foundation of your appearance, but you may not realize that the food choices you make can also affect how you look.

Maybe you have striking eyes or sparkling white teeth. Perhaps you have especially soft skin. Even if your features are not particularly striking, they can be enhanced by good health. Did you know that eating the right foods will increase the shininess of your hair and the strength of your nails? Proper diet also plays a large part in achieving the best figure you can attain given your particular build. Remember, even an attractive girl will not look good if she does not eat well.

The Two Meanings of "Diet"

It is very important to realize that there is a difference between the meaning of the word "diet" as it is used in the above paragraph and the kind of diet people go on to lose weight. When this book discusses how "health and diet" affect how you look and feel, it is referring to the amount and kinds of foods that you eat, not the type of diet that is discussed below.

Sandy's and Lily's Diets

Sandy was eighty pounds overweight. She couldn't even remember the last time she had seen a doctor. Sandy was ashamed of her eating habits. She loved to eat potato chips for breakfast and chocolate bars whenever she wanted a snack. Her favorite lunch, which she brought to school every day, was a fried peanut butter and honey sandwich on white bread. She was a fan of Elvis Presley's music, and she had read that this sandwich was one of his favorite snacks. Sometimes she would have two or three of them for lunch.

A friend of Sandy's, an extremely thin girl named Lily, suggested that Sandy see a nutritional specialist. Lily had needed to gain weight, so she went to a registered dietitian for help. The dietitian put Lily on a special diet to increase her weight. A registered dietitian is someone who has a college degree and a lot of experience in the field of nutrition. He or she also has passed a national examination and is registered with the American Dietetic Association (ADA).

Sandy told her mom that she wanted to lose weight and that she thought a dietitian would help, since she knew that she wasn't eating the right foods but didn't know how to start improving her eating habits. The dietitian told Sandy that he was going to put her on a low-fat diet. He said that Sandy ate far too much fat and that if she was careful about what she ate and exercised three times a week, she would soon begin to look and feel much better.

Healthy Eating Habits

More and more studies conducted by scientists and doctors confirm that a good diet improves health and helps us to look and feel our best. People like Sandy who eat too many fats and sweets can develop heart problems. People who don't eat enough, or are afraid to eat because they have an excessive fear of becoming fat, are in danger of developing eating disorders such as anorexia nervosa or bulimia nervosa. If you are concerned about your eating habits or those of someone you know, the Where to Go for Help section at the back of this book will aid you in finding more information.

Fitting Healthy Food Habits into Your Life

Many teens feel that because they are young and full of energy, they are invincible. To them, a healthy diet is something that only older people need to worry about. But the truth is that the sooner you develop healthy eating habits, the better off you will be for the rest of your life. It is helpful to think of healthy eating as a way of life instead of a tiresome detail that you need to find time for. Even when you're busy editing your high school paper, hanging out at the mall with your friends, thinking about the cute guy next door, or simply listening to music and twiddling your thumbs, you can still find the time to eat well. After all, if Erica can do it, so can you!

Erica seemed to be getting busier and busier every day. First there was the invitation to the junior prom. Nick, who was in Erica's music class, had invited her in the cutest way. He stuck a note in her guitar case that said "Erica, please be my prom date. Nick." She was so excited—especially when she thought about the pink satin gown she was going to sew all by herself. But then there was the Science Fair project that she had promised to help her stepbrother with. And the yoga classes she had started to take at the neighborhood YMCA. *And she had rehearsals to attend for her school's production of* West Side Story. *Plus, Erica had been on the honor roll every semester and she wasn't about to give it up now.*

How could she do all of this and maintain a healthy diet? Every Saturday, which was shopping day in her family, Erica and her dad made a list of all of the foods they would need for the following week. Erica made sure that she ate three meals a day. She never skipped breakfast because, as her grandmother used to tell her, "Breakfast food is brain food." For lunch, Erica liked to

Instead of eating greasy potato chips or cookies as after-school snacks, try low-fat foods such as fresh fruit or rice cakes.

have a healthy sandwich with not too much butter or mayonnaise—usually cheese and tomato or avocado and chicken—followed by some milk and a piece of fruit. Though a lot of the kids at school went to McDonald's for lunch, on most days Erica liked to save her allowance for other things. Still, on some days she did treat herself to fries or a sundae.

At dinner, Erica's family always started with a small appetizer, like carrots or celery with cream cheese; then they had pasta, fish, or chicken. For snacks, Erica liked to eat popcorn (with not too much butter or salt), apples, pretzels, or granola bars. Because she ate well and got enough sleep almost every night, Erica had the energy to balance all of her activities while still looking and feeling great.

Food for Thought

High-fiber, low-fat diets are recommended by most doctors and dietitians. Foods that are high in fiber include grains such as whole wheat, barley, corn, oats, and bran. Whole grains provide complex carbohydrates, which supply you with energy. They also give you vitamins and minerals. Most vegetables and fruits also contain fiber. Fiber helps to cleanse your digestive system and keep you from becoming constipated.

Most of us know that too much fat can clog arteries and cause weight gain. But a healthy diet does need to include some fat. So don't be afraid to eat the occasional piece of ice cream cake with warm chocolate sauce. The key is moderation—not too much and not too little. The same goes for sugary foods. If you like to snack a lot or if you often get cravings for something sweet, remember that fruit and frozen yogurt are sweet too! If you really want a candy bar, go ahead and have it. Just don't overdo it by eating a chocolate bar three times a day.

Our bodies also require vegetables and fruits. Aside from being a good source of fiber, they provide vitamins, minerals, and carbohydrates. Leafy greens like lettuce, spinach, and broccoli are especially good for us because they are an excellent source of calcium, which keeps our bones strong.

Meat, fish, poultry, eggs, and nuts are good sources of protcin, which provides energy and is essential for building muscle. If you are a vegetarian and decide not to eat any meat, you must be extra-careful to get enough protein. Beans, soy products, eggs, nuts, and peanut butter are excellent alternative sources of protein.

Milk and dairy products give you lots of calcium, which helps your bones to grow and stay strong. Calcium is also important for developing and maintaining strong teeth. Yogurt, cheese, and even ice cream will keep you healthy while you are growing. Eat low-fat or skim products whenever possible.

Liquids Are Important Too

Drinking plenty of fluids is essential for looking and feeling good. Water is best. It cleanses your system and hydrates your skin. Fruit juices are also good for you, if they are 100-percent natural and contain no added sugar. Look on the label of the container to find out if any artificial ingredients or sugar has been added. Milk provides you with lots of calcium. Drink low-fat or skim milk whenever possible. Watch out for sodas, most of which contain large amounts of sugar, as well as diet drinks or artificially flavored beverages, which may contain harmful chemicals.

Legal and Illegal Drugs

Putting poisons into your body is bad not only for your health but also for your appearance. Alcohol, believe it or not, is a poison. Small amounts can be cleansed from the body without doing any harm, but alcohol contains many calories and almost no nutritional value. Drinking large quantities of alcohol on a frequent basis can damage your liver, the organ that keeps your blood free of toxic substances. Other drugs, such as diet drugs, heroin, and speed, can be even more dangerous. Using them can cause people to lose their appetites and become severely malnourished. Once your body is in a weakened state, your immune system will not be in good working order and you will be at a higher risk of developing a serious illness.

Looking good involves much more than just your physical features. By developing a healthy lifestyle, which includes providing your body with good food, you are ensuring good health for now and the future.

Chapter 4

Keeping Fit

In the last chapter, we discussed how your diet plays a large role in determining how you look and feel. Food is not the only aspect of your daily life that is important in this respect. Proper exercise also contributes to your overall sense of well-being. Staying fit and healthy keeps your body in good working order, relieves stress, and keeps your mind alert.

You have probably seen many extremely well-toned models and actresses in magazines, on television, and in the movies. You may wonder how they always manage to look so perfect. Well, before you get upset and angry with yourself for not looking like they do, remember that looking good is a major part of the job of being a media star. Some actresses and models are naturally slim, but most have to exercise at least three to four hours a day in order to look the way they do. Most of us don't have that kind of time to spare. We have other interests and concerns that take priority over perfecting our looks. Also, don't forget that most celebrities have personal trainers, makeup artists, professional photographers, and hair-stylists to help them look glamorous at all times. More important, remember that no one type of body, face, or hair is "perfect." Everyone has his or her own taste and preferences. Also, personality plays a major role in how attractive someone appears.

Make sure that you set realistic goals for yourself when you start developing an exercise routine. If the word "exercise" conjures up unpleasant images of end-less aerobics classes or marathon runs, take a moment and examine your own daily routine. You may be sur-prised to find out that you already do a lot of exercise but you just weren't aware of it.

Healthy—and Fun—Activities

The following is a list of activities that are good for you:

- Taking a walk around your neighborhood by yourself or with your best friend, your signifi-cant other, or your dog.
- Walking up the stairs to your apartment, class-room, or place of worship.
- Playing frisbee in the park.
- Shopping at the mall. (Don't forget about all of that walking!)
- Kissing your significant other.

Outdoor exercise is a great way to keep fit, relieve stress, and clear your mind while getting some fresh air.

- Dancing at a club. Dancing is a great aerobic exercise that's also lots of fun. But remember that dancing in a smoky environment can be bad for your health, since you are breathing in poisonous air when your body needs pure air the most.
- Swimming at the pool or beach. Swimming is a good cardiovascular activity (one that strengthens your heart) and it gives your whole body a great workout.

If your idea of exercise is sitting in front of the television and giving your jaw a workout with a bag of extra-crunchy potato chips, you'll be happy to find that exercise can be fun and easy. If you are a serious athlete, however, or if you like the feeling of togetherness and group spirit that comes from being on a team, you may want to devote more time to one particular sport.

Melomie never thought she would play sports. She had four brothers who played soccer, but she was terrified of getting hit by the ball. Everything changed after she watched the World Cup. She loved watching Ronaldo, Dunga, and Bebeto—all of whom played on the Brazilian soccer team. Melomie even considered starting a Ronaldo fan club in her town, but she was worried that it would be useless since she knew nothing about the game—aside from how cute the players were.

"Hey, Melo, if you're so into Ronaldo, why don't you try playing soccer?" her brother Carlos asked. "You might really like it."

"Well, I guess I would really like to, but you guys are so rough and I don't want to get hit by the ball."

"We don't mean play with us, silly," said Maxie, Melomie's oldest brother. "You should play at school."

"But there is only a team for boys."

"So start a girls' team," Carlos suggested.

In the end, Melomie did form a girls' soccer team. She loved it! Running all over the field never seemed like hard work because she and the other girls were having such a good time. And she loved meeting the team members who played at neighboring schools. Eventually, Melomie grew to be such an expert at soccer that she did start the Ronaldo fan club.

You don't need to be wild about South American sports stars to become active in sports. Your school may have basketball, volleyball, swimming, softball, or dance teams. If you live in an area that gets a lot of snow in winter, you might want to try skating, skiing, or sledding. If your favorite sport isn't offered at your school, don't worry. There are plenty of other places that offer whatever sport or exercise interests you. Find out what types of activities are available at your local YMCA/YMHA, community center, or park. You may be able to rent or borrow the equipment you need from these places.

If you aren't interested in team sports, winter sports, or aerobics classes, you might want to try some of the different types of exercise that have become popular recently. Madonna, Demi Moore, Julia Roberts, and Drew Barrymore all practice yoga to keep fit. There are many different types of yoga, ranging from power yoga, which is similar to aerobics, to Hatha yoga, which primarily involves a series of slow stretching positions. Yoga tones and strengthens muscles, improves your balance, and relaxes you. That sounds pretty good, doesn't it? You may also want to try karate, kickboxing, spinning (superfast pedaling on a stationary bike), or tai chi. Look for these classes at community centers, YMCAs, or YMHAs.

It's great to exercise outdoors whenever possible. There is something about the fresh air and surrounding nature that clears the mind, soul, and body. Most cities have parks. If you live in the countryside, there

Julia Roberts, Drew Barrymore, Madonna, and Demi Moore all practice yoga to keep their minds and bodies fit—and you can too.

are roads and paths where you can walk or jog. Be sure to let a friend or relative know where you are and always exercise in a safe place. It is not a smart idea to run in a park after dark or to swim at a lake or in the ocean when there is no one nearby.

Exercising helps you take in more oxygen and makes your blood flow more freely. This process cleanses your body and keeps your organs and muscles in good shape. By exercising regularly, you run your blood through a filtering process that removes harmful waste particles from your system. Exercise brings in the clean oxygen your body needs to work properly. That is why people who are active are healthier. And when you are healthy, it shows.

Chapter 5

Liking the Person You See in the Mirror

As a teenager, you often have to deal with a lot of pressure to fit in. Kids at school may expect you to wear specific clothes and to look or speak a certain way. Magazines, movies, and TV shows send constant messages to use, buy, or try this kind of face cream, that brand of sneakers, or this type of shampoo. Maybe your parents, older siblings, or even your teachers are telling you to change your look. No wonder teens feel pressured! It's perfectly natural to feel overwhelmed by all of these mixed messages.

Try to remember that you are the person you see in the mirror. Learn to be happy with who you are and how you look. We are all born with certain features that were passed on to us by our parents. But while you are who you are—no matter what—there are some fun things you can do to play with or enhance your appearance.

Waseem

Waseem wanted to change how she looked. She wanted to fit in. Many of the girls in her school seemed to have red highlights in their hair. Waseem was from Pakistan and had jet black hair. After receiving an invitation to Ben's party, she decided that she would change her appearance for the occasion.

After looking through a few magazines, Waseem realized that for not too much money, she could give herself a whole new look. She went to a discount drugstore and stocked up on wash-out red highlights made especially for dark hair. She bought some pink lip gloss with a bit of glitter in it and found some cute nail decals too.

At the party, Waseem showed up with red highlights, a lot of makeup, and decorated nails. She was excited about her new appearance and couldn't wait to see what the other girls thought of her.

"Waseem!" screeched Paulette when she saw her friend. "You look great with red hair, but I really love your shiny black hair. You don't need the highlights."

"But you all have the same highlights," Waseem replied, confused.

"Maybe, but you're the only one with that beautiful black hair. My hair is so mousy. That's why I put color in it. If I had your hair, I wouldn't mess with it at all."

After that, Waseem spent less time thinking of what things she could do to change her appearance.

Hair Care

Different people have different types of hair. Waseem has thick hair that tends to get oily. Her friend Paulette has thin, dry hair. In order to find out which hair products are best for you, read the labels on shampoo and conditioner bottles. It is also wise to read the label to find out exactly what you are putting in your hair.

If you have dry hair, don't buy a shampoo for oily hair. Some products contain wax that builds up in your hair and makes it difficult to manage. Others may contain harsh chemicals. Also, if you are allergic to certain perfumes, make sure to buy unscented products. If a product causes your scalp to itch or your hair to fall out, stop using it immediately.

There are many hair products available that can enhance your look. You can try mousse or gel to add more body or to hold a particular style. You can do a home perm, change your hair color, or use glitter for a temporary touch of glamour.

Creme rinses and conditioners help to repair the damage caused by perms or coloring or to add moisture to naturally dry hair. Some people have very curly hair that can only be brushed when there is conditioner in it. If you usually blow-dry your hair, remember that hot air can cause split ends and may dry out the natural oils in your hair. Give your hair a break by letting it air-dry once in a while.

Have fun trying out different kinds of colorful hair clips, bands, and barrettes. The choices are endless.

Regularly washing your hair with shampoo and using a conditioner keeps your hair healthy and looking good.

Makeup

To keep your skin healthy and glowing, it's important to keep it clean. Be sure to check the ingredients in any soap, facial astringent, moisturizer, or mask that you use. Watch out for ingredients that might cause an allergic reaction. If you develop a rash or blemishes after trying a particular product, stop using it at once. It may be helpful to go to a dermatologist (a doctor specializing in skincare) if the problem persists.

You may want to try out different kinds of makeup at a drugstore or makeup counter. A makeup salesperson can show you how to use new products and can suggest which products work best with your particular features or skin type. However, beware of pushy salespeople who want you to purchase certain products. Never buy something unless you are sure that you want, need, and can afford it. Many salespeople urge you to buy expensive items because they work on commission, meaning that they receive a percentage of every sale they make.

The Price Is Right

Emme wanted to get the Poppy Red lipstick that her older sister wore. She found out what brand it was and went downtown to the department store. At the makeup counter, Emme noticed that one tube of the lipstick was twenty-one dollars. That was crazy! Her sister, Luisa, was a lawyer, so she could afford it, but not Emme. She had only three dollars.

Using makeup can be a fun way to add flair to your own personal style.

The saleswoman noticed the look of amazement on Emme's face and called her over to the counter.

"I'll tell you a secret," the saleswoman said. "If you go down to the bargain basement, they have their own brand of makeup. The packaging isn't as nice as ours, but the colors are practically the same."

"Oh, thanks," replied Emme.

When buying any item, whether it is a lipstick, a new dress, or a hair clip, remember to comparison shop. That way, you can make your dollars go further.

Every now and then, a new trend will come along that you may want to follow. Remember that these fads do not last long. Recently, it has become very popular to put designs on your skin. Instead of getting a tattoo, which can be expensive and painful—and very expensive to have removed when you no longer like it—try mehndi, or fake tattoos that you can wash off after a day.

Nails

You can further enhance your appearance with the proper care of your finger- and toenails. Your hands are always in public view, so you need to pay a lot of attention to them. Use a nail brush to scrub away the dirt that builds up under your nails. Also, trim your nails so that they aren't too long or ragged. You can use nail polish to add color to your hands; you may want to try nail decals to add a decorative touch.

As with hair care and skin products, watch out for anything that causes an allergic reaction. Some chemicals can damage your nails if you are allergic to them. Be especially careful with false nails. Extensive use of them can destroy the natural nail underneath.

Diet can improve the quality of your nails. As discussed in chapter two, calcium-rich foods make your nails stronger. The appearance of your nails also depends on your habits. If you bite or chew on your cuticles and nails, you need to stop! Keeping your nails clean is very important, since germs can collect under toe- and fingernails, causing odors, infections, and fungal diseases.

A comfortable, versatile look will boost your confidence and help you make a great first impression.

Fashion Follies

Fashion is a very important topic for most teen girls. You want to look your best, but styles are constantly changing, leaving you scrambling to keep up with the latest trends. But let's get one thing straight: You don't need to be a slave to fashion to look good and feel great.

If you can't afford the cashmere twin set that all the models are wearing, or if a short and sassy haircut is in and you're afraid that your long curls are out, stop worrying. Fashions will always change and there is nothing to gain from wasting your time, energy, money, and creativity on trying to be a follower. What's important is to wear clothing you like that both flatters you and that you feel comfortable in. Don't forget that you can *start* trends instead of following them. If you are a creative type with lots of innovative ideas, put your mind to work and see what you can come up with on your own. Here are some ideas:

- Can't afford the cashmere twin set? Try scouting out vintage or thrift stores where you can find fabulous sweater sets from the 1950s at discount prices. The Salvation Army, thrift shops, discount clothing stores, and flea markets often have great finds. And frequently you can come across big designer names too.
- Try adding a decorative touch to an old T-shirt, sweater, or shirt. Sew on antique buttons, ribbons, and lace that you find in fabric stores.

• If you have an old piece of clothing that isn't quite right, but you can't seem to part with it, try altering it to make something new. A long dress can be shortened to a mini. You can change the buttons, collar, and sleeve length of a long-sleeved shirt. Your favorite jeans that are tattered at the knees can be made into a great pair of cut-off shorts for the summer.

• Colors can be changed, so don't despair! With the help of some dye, that white shirt in your closet that has aged with time or the canary yellow sandals that you wore at your older sister's wedding could become your favorite fashion items. Fabric dye is available at most drugstores and works on almost any fabric. To be on the safe side, test the dye on a corner of whatever surface you want to transform. For a nice tea color, you can also dye your old white clothes in a tub of tea. Just boil some water, add a few tea bags, and drop in your old white shirt for fifteen to twenty minutes.

• If you have an artistic side, you can buy fabric paints or glitter and paint designs of your own.

To Sum It All Up . . .

You don't need to succumb to peer pressure to be fashionable and look good. Remember that some occasions may call for a more pulled together look, but in

Taking the extra time to find clothes at discount stores can save you a lot of money.

general, just be yourself. If you have read this book carefully, you should now have a better understanding of why it is important to take care of yourself—your skin, your teeth, your hair, your facial and verbal expressions, your clothing, and your attitude. In a nutshell, good grooming and hygiene skills are essential as they will help carry you through life while ensuring that you are at your best!

Glossary

acne A skin disorder that causes pimples on the face and sometimes also on the back and chest.

anorexia nervosa/bulimia Two of the most common eating disorders, both characterized by an obsession with being overweight.

blackheads Pimples caused by oil, secreted by glands, which turns black when exposed to air.

dandruff Tiny scales of dry skin from the scalp.

dental floss Nylon thread used to clean between the teeth.

dietitian A doctor who specializes in healthy eating and nutrition.

dermatologist A doctor who specializes in treating skin disorders.

fluoride A chemical found in drinking water and toothpaste that keeps teeth strong.

halitosis Bad breath.

hygiene Practices that promote and maintain health, such as cleanliness.

plaque A sticky film that forms on the surface of the teeth and can lead to decay.

pores Millions of tiny openings in the skin.

tai chi Ancient Chinese meditation exercises.

yoga A system of exercises aimed at producing and enhancing mental and spiritual well-being.

For Further Reading

Bailey, Sheril. *The Sheril Bailey Complete Manicuring and Nailcare Guide.* Kansas City, MO: Andrews & McMeel, 1998.

Carpenter, Dana, and Woody Winfree, eds. *I Am Beautiful: A Celebration of Women in Their Own Words.* Bridgeport, CT: Rose Communications, 1996.

Cooke, Kaz. *Real Georgeous: The Truth About Body and Beauty.* New York: W. W. Norton & Co., 1996.

Frankenberger, Elizabeth. *Food and Love: Dealing with Family Attitudes About Weight.* New York: Rosen Publishing Group, 1998.

Gordon, Marsha, and Alice E. Fugate. *The Complete Idiot's Guide to Beautiful Skin.* Old Tappan, NJ: Macmillan Publishing, 1998.

Krizmanic, Judy. *A Teen's Guide to Going Vegetarian.* New York: Viking Books, 1994.

Price, Deirdra. *Healing the Hungry Self: The Diet-Free Solution to Lifelong Weight Management.* New York: Plume, 1998.

Quant, Mary. *Classic Makeup and Beauty.* New York: D K Publishing, 1996.

Reybold, Laura. *Everything You Need to Know About the Dangers of Tattooing and Body Piercing.* New York: Rosen Publishing Group, 1998.

Salter, Charles A. *The Nutrition-Fitness Link: How Diet Can Help Your Body and Mind.* Brookfield, CT: Millbrook Press, 1993.

Seymour, Stephanie. *Beauty Basics for Dummies.* Indianapolis, IN: I D G Books, 1998.

Shandler, Sarah. *Ophelia Speaks: Adolescent Girls Write About Their Search for Self.* New York: HarperCollins, 1999.

Where to Go for Help

Organizations

In the United States

American College of Nutrition
c/o Hospital for Joint Diseases
301 East 17th Street
New York, NY 10003
(212) 777-1037

American Dietetic Association
216 West Jackson Boulevard
Chicago, IL 60606-6996
(800) 877-1600
Web site: http://www.eatright.org

Young Men's Christian Association (YMCA) of the USA
101 North Wacker Drive
Chicago, IL 60606
(312) 977-0031
Web site: http://www.ymca.net

In Canada

Dietitians of Canada
480 University Avenue, Suite 604
Toronto, Ontario M5G 1V2
(416) 596-0857
Web site: http://www.dietitians.ca

Food Institute of Canada
415-1600 Scott Street
Ottawa, Ontario KIY 4N7
(613) 722-1000
Web site: http://www.foodnet.fic.ca

Health Canada
A.L. 0913A
Ottawa, Ontario K1A 0K9
(613) 957-2991
Web sites: http://www.hc-sc.gc.ca (english)
          http://www.he-sc.gc.ca (français)

Young Men's Christian Association (YMCA) of Canada
42 Charles Street East, 6th Floor
Toronto, Ontario M4Y 1T4
(416) 967-9622
Web site: http://www.ymca.ca/home.htm

Web Sites

Chick Click
http://www.chickclick.com

Girl Power
http://www.girlpower.com
Encourages and motivates adolescent girls, specifically
through writing.

Girls, Inc.
http://www.girlsinc.org
Official Web site for the national organization Girls, Inc.

gURL
http://www.gurl.com
Humorous yet realistic look at sex, emotions, body image,
relationships, and more. Also offers free e-mail.

KidsHealth
http://www.kidshealth.org/teen/nutrition/index.html

Nutrition Cafe
http://nutrition.central.vt.edu

Nutrition on the Web for Teens
http://library.advanced.org/10991

Teen.com
http://www.teen.com

Teenspeak
http://www.teenspeak.com
Information on fashion, music, movies, relationships, boys,
sex—you name it!

Ten Tips to Eating Healthy and Physical Activity
http://ificinfo.health.org/brochure/10tipkid.htm

The World According to Girl!
http://www.girlson.com
Girls on film, girls on books, and more.

You Are What You Eat: A Guide to Good Nutrition
http://library.advanced.org/11163/gather/cgi-bin/
   wookie.cgi

On-line Teen Magazines

BLAST!
http://www.blastmag.com/main.html

react.com
http://www.react.com

teenzine
http://members.xoom.com/tznet

Index

About the Author

Annie Leah Sommers is a young adult book editor and a printmaker. She holds a master's degree in children's literature and one in secondary education. Annie has an older brother named Michael and a cat named Jesse

Photo Credits

Cover Photograph © Steve Skjold/Skjold Photographs. P. 42 by Karen Tom; p. 46 by Brian T. Silak; pp. 22, 51 Simca Israelian; p. 22, 39 by John Bentham; p. 48 by Chris Volpe; p. 6 by Bonnie Rothstein Brewer; all other photos by Dru Nadler.